Confessions of a Christian Woman in Leadership

Confessions of a Christian Woman in Leadership

What Every Woman in Leadership Should Know

Diana Graham

Confessions of a Christian Woman in Leadership

Copyright © 2015 by Diana Graham

All rights reserved. No part of this book may be reproduced or transmitted in any form or by any means without written permission from the author.

Worldwide Publishing Group
Your multi-platform publishing partner
7710-T Cherry Park Drive, Suite 224, Houston, Texas 77095
www.WorldwidePublishingGroup.com
(713) 766-4272

eBook ISBN: 978-1-312-46677-7

Paperback ISBN: 978-0692346549

Hard Cover ISBN: 978-1-312-46675-3

Table of Contents

Foreword *7*

Dedication *9*

Introduction *11*

Chapter One **Ambassador-Kingdom of God** *15*

Chapter Two **Apostolic Vision** *25*

Chapter Three **Supernatural Gifts**..........................*39*

Chapter Four **Innovative Leadership/ Making Disciples** *47*

Chapter Five **Apostolic Team Building** *59*

Chapter Six **Sending and Releasing** *63*

Chapter Seven **Practical Application** *65*

Chapter Eight **Next Steps** *73*

Addendum *79*

Diana's Ministry Related Bio: *81*

Contact the Author..*84*

Foreword

What a privilege to work alongside Diana Graham in God's kingdom. If you did not know her story, you would never suspect what she's been through to garner all the wisdom she offers in this book. Nobody has the right to remain in a victim status after reading her book, no matter what challenge life is throwing at them. Diana doesn't just repackage what she heard or read from somebody else. She shows true leadership, offering turn-by-turn navigation through the confrontations present in the lives of her readers.

In her current chapter of life, Diana is once again employing many of the truths she has learned in earlier stages, as she pioneers an area of ministry for her local church. A passion for the homeless and those who are economically challenged has driven Diana to use skills she mastered in corporate America to design and orchestrate the efforts of a team that will train, coach and provide resources to those in need. I'm sure it has not been as easy as Diana makes it look, but it is evident that God has graced her to be a model of what He could do though you, too!

Anthony E. Cox, Lead Pastor
Relevant Life Church, Lewisville, TX

Dedication

This book is dedicated to my mom, Virginia Graham. As a woman of God, mom influenced everyone for Jesus; my mom knew and loved God. My mother had unwavering **God faith** even under devastating circumstances. She never demonstrated anger at God through, or as a result of, her bad experiences. During all of the trials, she had divine faith. I asked God to let her know I have written this book as she is now with the Lord. Mom is honored and I know she would be pleased.

This book is dedicated to all the pastors who made Jesus Lord of their lives and God used to change and influence my life; *Frankie and John Kuffel, Marti and Sherman Williams, Emmanuel Cannistraci, Lindell Bennett, JoAnn and Chet Gallagher, Carol and Chris Cobb, Jennifer and Chuck Boone, Marge' and Jack Brandt, Daniel Clubb, Jodi and Jeff Harris.* Their leadership, encouragement and motivation led me to follow Christ and to acknowledge who I am in Christ, thus wrecking the plans of the enemy for my life. Thank you for your Jesus impact on my life, your guidance and your obedience to God's call.

Thank you to my family and friends; for your confidence and support during the good times and the not so good times. I also want to thank Mrs. Catherine Hastings, and Mrs. Donna Stroop for your much needed editing skills. May God's love and His grace continue to abide in you and bless you! Love y'all.

- Diana

Introduction

"**Lessons Learned,**" in project management terms, is a list of both good and bad results and issues. Results and issues that the team collects during the project, when the project is completed, the list is shared and reviewed with the team.

There is a spirit of sharing with the team. The goal is to inform the next team starting a similar project so that they may use the process that resulted in the success stories and not make any of the same mistakes. The "lessons learned" concept is a great tool for ministry. The ministry team review of programs, mission trips, etc.

My hope is that this book is a catalyst for all Christian leaders to encourage the entire body of Christ to serve God. Encourage everyone to use all of their gifts, skills and experiences to positively impact and **train** others. **The God influence in our leadership role impacts us everywhere we participate in life, with no limitations at home, in the workplace, at school, among friends and with our colleagues.**

My Journey

I researched the Bible to locate where a woman could have apostolic gifts and where she could be an apostle. In Dr. David Cannistraci's book "The Gift of Apostle", Dr. Cannistraci mentions that Junia was most likely a woman. Paul mentions in Romans that Junia was among the apostles. I asked Chrisoula, my Greek friend, to please look for Junia in her Greek Bible and to let me know if Junia was a woman. The New King James version: Romans 16:7 "Greet Andronicus and **Junia**, my countrymen and my fellow prisoners, who are *of note among the apostles*, who also were in Christ before me." In place of "note," in other translations, the words used are outstanding or prominent among the apostles.

While traveling to Greece and exploring the footsteps of Paul, I was blessed to meet Chrisoula, my Greek roommate; she is first generation born in the USA. Chrisoula's response to my inquiry; "Yes, Junia is absolutely female. In the Greek Bible, the title before the names referenced are; "ton androniko and tin Iounia" the title word "ton" refers to males and the title "tin" is used to refer to females. We have scripture to support that Junia was, in fact, a woman and according to the Apostle Paul, she was an apostle. In fact, some biblical scholars even believe Junia may be the author of Hebrews.

Chrisoula also researched the scripture in 1 Timothy 2:12 where Paul recorded; *"do not permit a woman to teach or to assume authority over a man; she must be quiet."* In the Greek Bible the word that was originally translated "man" in English actually is referring to a husband. According to Biblical scholars and in the context this letter was written to the Corinthian church, leads us to believe that during this time period, the Corinthian women were not educated. They were raised to be wives and mothers. So, for instance, when they attended Paul's teaching and Paul made reference to "one" God, they had questions!

In Grecian teaching there were many gods. Their reaction was based on their culture's polytheism teaching; their belief system was shaken and their illiteracy provoked questions, which disrupted the general session. Paul was telling the men to go home, teach and educate their wives; not only in what Paul taught but also to teach them how they should listen and not disrupt the teaching. They should hold their questions until they get home.

My Prayer

I pray that the women God has called into Christian leadership will hear and understand the direction and the importance of their leadership contribution within the kingdom of God.

In this book I share my experiences from growing up in church and from a business perspective as a divorced

Christian woman. I have been successful in business leadership for over 25 years and have also had mixed experiences in leadership roles in the church My purpose in authoring this book is in obedience to what I believe God has called me to share. I hope to reach women called by God to an apostolic leadership role in the kingdom of God.

God does not disqualify you because you are a woman, nor is He limited in whom He chooses to call and ordain as His leaders. If God has called you to an apostolic leadership role, if you have the heart for making disciples, mentoring and building leaders, He may choose to place mentees-disciples in your life for you to train and to love. There is nothing about being a woman that should disqualify you or talk you out of your call by God.

Chapter One
Ambassador-Kingdom of God

Purposed to serve God

In August of 1992, I rededicated my life to Christ. It had been a very difficult six years of struggling with the failure of my marriage and becoming a divorced Christian. A divorced Christian is something I never wanted to become. In fact, I considered it to be an oxymoron. In the fall of 1998, Pastor Emmanuel Cannistraci preached that divorce is not an unforgivable sin. I was immediately set free and I started the process to legally change my last name back to my maiden name. The transformation within me was amazing as the guilt and shame were permanently removed. I graduated from Bible College in December of that year using my maiden name.

My Journey

My divorce in 1986 brought a great deal of shame and hurt into my life. My husband and I met with our pastor at the time; we were experiencing financial difficulties with -$79 in our joint checking account. I knew my returning to work was the only answer. My biggest concern at this time was leaving my almost three year old daughter in daycare. The pastor's response to us was, "Diana you should not go back to work, if you do, the men you work with will find you attractive and you will leave your husband". As we left the church office my thought at this time was he is an idiot (forgive my honesty) and he has no idea who I am. He had projected on our situation what he had experienced. He was a gifted evangelist but obviously, his gift was not a pastor-counselor.

My pastor's concern that I might have an issue with fidelity didn't make any sense to me; however I now look back and remember my ex-husband's comment; that my career was more important to me then he was. He blamed my focus on work for our marital issues. Brokenheartedly, I have accepted and asked forgiveness for my contribution to the demise of our seventeen years of marriage.

Starting three years after my divorce (December of 1989–August of 1992), I experienced the trials of trying to learn how to date again and to be a single mom. What a disaster! I dated a different man every three months. I knew the failure of my marriage was no excuse for my behavior as my hurt turned into anger. I know I hurt people during this time period and I have repented. I quickly found I needed to focus on being a mom. Single parenting is not easy, however, it was fulfilling and we had some fun. I consider my daughter good fruit and truly a joy in my life.

It was obvious my life's choices were not pleasing to God. It had become very clear to me that if I did not change my direction, I was going to die, if not physically, certainly I was dying spiritually. One Sunday at Fremont Community Church, as Marti Williams played the piano after the message; I rededicated my life to Christ. That day my life forever changed. I have lifelong covenant friends I met during my three years at FCC. I spent this time reconnecting with God and His people.

April 9th of 1995 I was dating a gentleman who was at the time my best friend. During a difficult time in my relationship with a close family member, he suggested I needed to go to a church that he assured me had a different relationship with God.

Imagine my surprise when I walked into Evangel Christian Fellowship that Sunday evening and was hit like a bolt of lightning by God's Holy Spirit. I received a prophetic word from Pastor Emmanuel Cannistraci (now referred to as Apostle Emmanuel Cannistraci). I saw the Shekinah glory of God and I smelled Jesus. I didn't know what these experiences were; all I knew then is that it was God. My life has never been and will never be the same!

I was a sponge over the next three years, learning and experiencing the miracles of God, the power of God, and the healing of God. I was healed both miraculously and through deliverance. In the next couple of months, I asked for and was filled with the baptism of the Holy Spirit. It was amazing! I describe the transformation in receiving the Holy Spirit like an enhanced super power in my spiritual gifts. It was like going from a 9V battery to 220V. I gave my heart to Jesus when I was in third grade in Bethel Christian Academy; I was nine. I have had spiritual gifts as long as I can remember, however, now my gifts were enhanced and more real, I knew then as I know now, I have more of God.

God's Representative

My attitude in the workplace was impacted by my growing understanding and my relationship with Christ. I have always been a leader and a visionary. Many comment I am a dreamer. Some of my family members I know at times have found it annoying and have felt this has impacted my ability to accept or to operate in reality. My view of life is impacted by my ability to see potential in most people. I see beyond the circumstances of most people and I see the good in them when others cannot. This may be why I appear to have no fear. I am seemingly, at times, not impacted by limitations or attitudes of man.

I know there is a greater purpose for all of us. We just need to get closer to God, to recognize and to realize our purpose. Life in this flesh and life in general is the distraction. These distractions can keep us from our purpose in God. It could in part be what Paul mentions to the Corinthians when he said that he died daily. *"I affirm, brethren, by the boasting in you whom I have in Christ Jesus our Lord, I die daily"* (1 Corinthians 15:31).

Lesson Learned:

Partnership with God requires constant communication with Him.

Love

Jesus added only one commandment; *we must love each other*. If we truly love God and if we love our neighbor as we do ourselves, we would not have any issues with unity; there would be no wars. However we do not love our neighbors as we should. My drive and ambition is apparent in most everything I do, but I learned in representing God, we must always be motivated in love.

Listening

I learned the importance of listening while attending a seminar I refer to as "charm school". We must listen to those we lead, even if we do not think there is value in what this person has to say, even if we don't value their input as it seems to be based on a lack of known expertise. If a person is an expert, we accept their credibility in what they share. In leadership we need to listen and discern so that we better understand their perception and why it is important to them. If we don't listen to those we lead, we are telling them that they do not matter. If we do not listen, we do not understand the person's perceptions. If we represent God and are His leaders, the people we lead need to matter to us!

We may say all people are important; however if our actions do not display we care, we are revealing what is really in our hearts. In partnership with God my heart should reflect the heart of Jesus. Everyone is important to Jesus.

Goals and Vision

I learned early in my career about the importance of documenting a vision. Your five year plan, goals and a charter are keys to success. I did not realize then how Biblically sound this instruction was, as it did not come from a Godly person nor was it presented as a Biblical concept. It is wonderful to recognize how practical the Bible is and how wonderful God has provided our daily life instruction manual. The Bible should be used in all aspects of our lives.

Since my mid-thirties I have a documented vision and have set goals. Some have been realized. With God, most accomplishments exceed the goals originally set. I have learned when we pray, we partner with God. We pray to capture the vision and to set our goals, with God. Our direction is to let God lead with our hands open, understanding we cannot own the goal nor should we hold on too tightly to our perceptions. If we are open to Him and we allow God to direct the path, we will then, not only realize His goals, but the achievements of our goals can be even better than what was originally set.

Visions and goals provide direction, we need a vision. As the Bible states, without a vision we will perish. Even if we never reach a five year plan or achieve every goal. However, if we have the right heart and clear daily direction from God, we are on a path that will lead to achievement and ultimate success. We need to be compelled to stick to the path God has for us. I know the Israelites had a clear direction and a vision toward getting to the promise land. However their hearts were not right. Vision, goals, purpose and a charter will not be of benefit if your heart is not right with God. I am not suggesting you stop. I am suggesting you simply ask God to check your heart. God has a way of correcting us as we go; and He will stop us if we listen, and if, He deems it necessary.

Clear Individual Direction

Growing up with a prophetic mother that was very discerning and then studying under the leadership of Pastors Chris and Carol Cobb, I learned so much about my gift of discernment, about prayer, and about how prophetic intercession and warfare work with God. These gifts are what lead to setting us, His people, free.

Finding Your Ministry

I was so excited and free, with what I learned during my time spent in healing and deliverance ministry. In the first Freedom Clinic meeting I attended, Pastor Chris said, "Right now someone is being delivered from a spirit of unforgiveness". I felt claws in my shoulders release and a great peace came over me. I wanted to get a rope and hog tie people and drag them in to get prayer. Pastor Chris is so wise. He shared with me, Jesus never looked for ministry; <u>ministry found Him</u>. I thought at one point healing was my ministry. I shared this with Pastor Chris and his input was "no, healing is a part of your ministry but it is not your only ministry". What a relief! Healing ministry is not always a lot of fun. It is rewarding but it can become burdensome, it was wonderful to learn the healing ministry was not a pinnacle for me. There is more that God has in store for my ministry, my life!

In Transition

I also learned there is no pinnacle or ultimate goal within our service in Christ. We are always growing and always learning. A common comment is that we are in transition. My response is when are we not in transition? Yes there are more intense moments and seasons. However, transition is the position of a Christian. In my experience, if we are too comfortable, we become stagnant and we don't need God as much. My challenge and yours, too, is keeping our eyes on Jesus so we can continue walking on the water.

Key Characteristics of Women with Apostolic gifts are specifically a trainer of trainers and a leader of leaders. I asked the Lord for His words for this book. "I need to know what you, God, are asking me to share from my experiences." He reminded me of the ministries I have helped start; the people we have loved, prayed for and with those we have trained, mentored, spoken to prophetically, and those we have corrected in love. OK Lord! Let's write this book.

Chapter Two
Apostolic Vision

Unshakeable Faith Building Dreams

Not all of the dreams and the visions I have documented and experienced are what would be considered successful or appreciated. However, they have certainly been educational. During the last year of Bible College and the year after graduating, a team from Evangel Christian Fellowship started home groups in Fremont. With the intention we would at some point start a church. We had passion to please God and to bring more of Him into Fremont. After all once you finish Bible College aren't you supposed to start a church? Isn't a church plant what people do when they graduate?

At the peak of our home ministry groups there were three good sized, fruitful, home groups. The numbers were promising, people were learning about Christ and accepting Him as their Lord, receiving healing, learning how to minister to each other and how to lead lives pleasing to God. It was great for a couple of years, but toward the end, the people moved on (some physically) and the vision diminished. Were we wrong? Did we not hear from God?

Was it timing? All good questions, I don't have the answers. All I know is that lifelong relationships were rooted during this time. The covenant relationships formed then continue to bless me now.

I have no regrets and I know God's hand was and still is on all of us. I can say my faith in God did not diminish. My understanding grows as I accept God's timing is perfect and He knows what is best for all of us. This is more apparent as my awareness of God continues to increase. My concern at the time was, did I somehow miss something; and more importantly, did I disappoint God? I have learned since then that God is so much bigger than my perceived failures. I now know beyond a shadow of a doubt that if it had been God's will to start a church at that time, we would have started a church. In retrospect, if I was a leader in a conventional church, I would have missed the experiences I had in my 12 year's tenure in consulting and working in Information Technology for a contract manufacturer. I would have missed the lifelong covenant relationships, extensive travel, meeting, loving, teaching, praying for, and learning from many diverse cultures.

When something does not go my way, I now try to stop, back up and not blame the other party(s). I am confident it is God placing His will for me on their hearts as well as in my heart. I would have missed out on so much of this world I have now had the blessing and the privilege to explore. I understand the favor that was and is upon my life is God and all of this is a part of my apostolic call and training.

During my years as an IT Director, I had one experience after leading someone to the Lord and then later having to formally correct this person and then ultimately dismissing him as I was then directed by upper management. This was very difficult, but quickly I learned as a leader, I am under greater scrutiny. I learned how I must always be sure my words and my actions honor God. In an altercation with this person, I called him a less than godly name. It did come back to me through the human resource department.

When asked if I had accused him of being the backside of a donkey, I had to respond truthfully. Yes, I had responded to him in frustration, however, what he said was true. I confessed it was a wrong response I regretted (even if his behavior at the time prompted the response-yes, I failed that test). I learned very quickly my actions were being observed at a higher level and if I cannot honor God, I need to go home, shut the door, and get right with Him before I open my mouth or do anything that would dishonor Him and dishonor and embarrass myself.

Living with Purpose

My daughter married and moved out of my home the year before I started Bible College. It was a tough transition time for me. My purpose as a mom was no longer required. I was truly a fish out of water. I praise God for the next few years I had with Stephanie. Steph is my first spiritual daughter and the first person God placed in my life to love and disciple/mentor. When she moved in with me, she quickly became a much needed joy. Steph has amazing spiritual gifts. She is a visionary, with amazing prophetic gifts. Her faith and her zeal for God are like no other. God is first in Steph's life. She and her family, a husband and four small children, continue to be a part of my life and are an incredible blessing to me.

Soon after joining Evangel Christian Fellowship I was asked to join the prayer team. I attended the Friday evening prayer team training led by Pastors Chris and Carol Cobb. We had prayer training on Friday evenings and then one Friday a month we led and participated in the deliverance ministry, the "Freedom Clinic".

I reduced the standard 40 hours to 36 in my job so that I could spend ministry time in the church on Fridays.

I assisted Pastor Chris with the administration support, doing statistical reporting for small groups. A few months later he asked me to lead the Freedom Clinic. We began to schedule a prayer time on Friday afternoons with individuals seeking healing and deliverance ministry. This was a period of time I had the greatest joy as I learned about God's heart in the ministry of prayer. There is nothing more powerful and rewarding than healing and deliverance ministry.

A life altering experience and an incredible blessing for me was when Pastor Chris asked me to help start and to oversee the SARAH Ministry. One of the church members had experienced so much healing and deliverance that she had a vision for a ministry for women, women that had been sexually abused as children. Mary had lost a baby she named Sarah so she wanted the ministry name to be in her memory. We met, prayed, and came up with the acronym of **S**exual **A**buse **R**ecovery **A**nd **H**ealing. Immediately, the SARAH Ministry was and still is a blessed and fruitful ministry. The ministry is still active today in Gateway City Church (formally Evangel Christian Fellowship) in San Jose, California.

When Pastor Chris approached me, I was not sure how I could start a ministry in an area I had no experience. Mary asked me if I had ever experienced sexual abuse. "No," was my response. She said I was really blessed. I told her I had an issue with saying I was blessed as that meant she was not blessed, because of what she had experienced. I told her I don't believe that is how God works. I believe this was just an area the enemy had not found a way to use against me. We know John 10:10 says, *"The thief does not come except to steal, and to kill, and to destroy."* In 1 Peter 5: 8 we read, *"Be sober, be vigilant; because your adversary the devil walks about like a roaring lion, seeking whom he may devour"* (in the Greek, the word devour can also be interpreted as distract or preoccupy). The devil has used plenty of other areas to work toward my destruction and distraction.

I soon realized the women with history of this abuse would have struggled to start this ministry. It would be tough to go through the intense healing while trying to lead others through the inner healing process. I sat through the first series of "The Wounded Heart"; I worked with our leaders and the new leaders of SARAH to document and set the ground rules of the SARAH Ministry group.

We first emphasized in a written contract, anonymity is required to make this a safe place, a place to share within the group their experiences. This began their much needed healing. As I listened and prayed, I cried most of the time. This time truly knitted our hearts together. It was a time that each participant shared the painful circumstances of their abuse. I learned about real humiliation and the worse kind of betrayal children can experience; the betrayal of parents and caregivers. As each story revealed the lack of protection from their mothers, I realized that this area of intense evil brings destruction within a seed that in most cases appears to be rooted within many families.

I was stunned at what I heard and heartbroken for the women that seemed to be unprotected by their families and, in some cases, were abused by their biological father among other family members. I remember thinking about my teenage years and what a pain my mother was, so protective and smothering. After my experience in starting this ministry, I thanked my mom for teaching me at a young age about sexual predators. I continue to thank God for my mom and for her faith and leading us to a closer relationship with Jesus. I thanked God for my father, for not only loving me unconditionally, but for protecting me. I was able to ask mom and God for their forgiveness for not appreciating mom's Godly example.

As the ministry lead, I worked with the SARAH leaders to setup the formal written agreements that each participant acknowledged by signing. I met with the SARAH leaders as a team and individually to coach, counsel, and to correct as was necessary. There were leaders that in their zealousness to encourage change in the lives of their participants were not in agreement with some of the direction and guidelines Pastor Chris had outlined for the SARAH team. I counseled with them that, while we don't have to agree with our leaders, we must do as the leaders ask as obedience is very important in our leadership role. We cannot expect blessing if we are rebelling against our leaders, even if the situation seems to be God and the rebellion is not intentional. The issue was whether to minister deliverance in an open session of SARAH or to take the person aside and pray and counsel with her independently. This made obedience seem secondary. The perception is that when there is demonic manifestation, the timing for deliverance ministry should be immediate. However, this is when discernment is essential; the enemy can and will use ministry time to distract and to hurt people. Waiting for a private time is in most cases preferable to then focus on the healing and deliverance of the person.

One of our SARAH leaders and I worked together for a few weeks on the Biblical and the practical reasoning for obedience. It became obvious that she was going to continue to find ways to push me away. I didn't know what to say or do to help get this point across. I finally told her "It does not matter what you do, you can do nothing that will make me not love you". I knew this had to be God speaking through me as the impact was immediate and it spoke to both of us. Suddenly the misunderstanding was defused and she knew that she was loved and supported by her leadership. The transformation was immediate and we became a great team as we worked together to serve the ministry, the SARAH Ministry reaches and heals the souls of many hurting people. I learned childhood sexual abuse (CSA) is an area that the enemy uses to destroy so many lives, both female and male. Lives are impacted daily by sexual abuse.

Statistics show that one in five girls and one in six boys have experienced childhood sexual abuse. Children are most vulnerable to CSA between the ages of seven and thirteen. Over the course of their lifetime approximately 28 percent of people have experienced some measure of CSA. Most experiences were between the ages of 14 and 17. We learned in many cases that the perpetrator was also a victim as a child. Some husbands of the women participating in the ministry approached the SARAH Ministry leads and thanked them for the ministry. They shared with joy and gratitude as to how the SARAH Ministry had helped to transform their marriages.

I loved the SARAH team and was so blessed to help them get this ministry started. I learned so much about women whom are wounded and hurting. I began to understand and recognize the symptoms. It really helped me to minister to women and to be a better friend. Women have not always been very good to me. It really helped me to see another side of women and to begin to see there may be a place in my heart for women.

I could also see why the enemy had placed the "not so nice" women in my life in the early stages of my career. The enemy's job is to steal, to kill and to destroy. He is focused on destroying our joy, our love for each other, and our ministry call from God. However, as we grow in our relationship with Christ we find all things do work together for good, as we learn from our disappointments, our hurt and our failures. We can become a person with purpose and direction which includes the relationships that we need to become better people.

My Plans for the Future

I had a vision once that when I completed my secular career/job that part of my retirement plan was to start or be a part of a nonprofit, possibly a consulting firm. This firm could consist of people with marketable skills, skills providing a service to the business community. The consultants would receive compensation based on what they need or a matrix to be determined. The nonprofit would place the profits in a fund. This fund would provide support for children's education. These children would have proven that they have the drive to pursue academically what could contribute toward better lives for themselves and their families.

I have a burden for children's education, especially with the challenges in funding for education in California. I can see that this is and is going to continue to be a great need. It could be that the participating consultants would determine the recipients of the funds based on what they contribute. It appears this vision is not God's vision for my future. God is asking me to reset my plans for retirement. My focus is on ministry. He will provide the money. God is my provider. I thought the vision was good and it made sense; however I realize it is not God for me, I am relieved. If the activity, job, or ministry is God, it will contain His favor, His fruit, and He will provide.

Organization is critical in an apostolic role. Leading a ministry team is comparable to leading a business team. The founding pastor can be comparative to a CEO, Chief Executive Officer. The responsibility of the leadership and administration of the ministry can be among the duties of an administrative pastor. The founding pastor, if an evangelist, may not have a gift of administration. He/she can delegate this role as part of an apostolic team type partnership. In a business, it is not unusual for an engineer to start a business. If wise, he/she will know their strengths and weaknesses within the business structure. Many then engage with those who have a similar passion for the product or service with complementing skills, gifts, and/or talents.

In ministry this may also include networking for advertising the ministries, funding, leading fund raisers (for missions additional ministries not covered with tithing) and the oversight of the financials. Today the management of the web site is another very key role. Most roles can be delegated based on the strength of the founder and the leading participants within the ministry. The head or lead pastor must recognize his/her strengths. He/she would do well to connect with associate pastors who would fill the required job roles covering their weaknesses or areas either they do not have the time for or are simply not experienced or as gifted.

Ministry Focus

A ministry's vision of equipping the body of Christ, training leaders while building apostolic ministry teams, should be a key focus. The operation's responsibilities within a ministry include, but are not limited to training, managing and publishing the organizational charts. This includes the roles of the ministry team's leaders. The Lord is over all of the

Church. The gifts He gave to perfect the saints for the work of the ministry are found in Eph. 4:11. They are Apostle, Prophet, Evangelist, Pastor and Teacher. These positions, which are often referred to as the fivefold ministry gifts, can correlate to a typical corporate structure CEO (head pastor), COO (Executive Pastor), CFO (Chief Financial Officer/Treasurer) Human Resources and Administration, Sales/Marketing (Evangelism). The combination of the gifts and experience of a team should have the potential to include all of the Eph. 4:11 gifts. Each team lead is responsible for the goals and objectives for their team. These goals and objectives should be in support of the ministry's vision and mission.

Organizational Charts

The organizational charts for each team would delineate the hierarchy of the ministry, including the pastoral oversight, and would reveal each function within the ministry. Each team lead would be responsible for the training schedules and a metrics for the ministry, identifying the apostolic team members and a communications team responsible for the monthly and quarterly updates of the newsletters and the website.

Organizational team members are identified by their supporting passions. As they have exhibited their ability by their talents and spiritual gifts. The ministry participants/team members define their duties in support of the ministry. Ministry team objectives should include the training schedules and their metrics KPIs (Key Performance Indicators) for the ministry. The team would identify the apostolic team members and a project communications team responsible for the monthly and quarterly updates of the project related documents and publications.

In Breath of Heaven, the Operations Team was responsible for the budgets, both operational and project specific. We were also responsible for the project updates/reporting including, project plans for the scheduling and the drilling of wells, supervising the building of a children's home, leading of mission trips, and scheduling the team training. The ministry team training was practical ministry training. There are samples of subjects listed in the appendix.

Chapter Three
Supernatural Gifts

Our Spiritual Gifts are imparted in us when we acknowledge Jesus Christ is the Lord of our lives. After we acknowledge our acceptance of Jesus Christ, it takes time for our spiritual gifts to mature. Salvation is just the beginning of our relationship with God in Christ. Pastor Jeff Harris recently taught that it was 14 years after Saul's conversion before he began his ministry. Paul (Saul prior to his conversion) met Jesus on the road to Damascus and consequently lost his sight. God told Ananias to go to Paul to bring healing to him. *It was 14 years later that Paul begins his ministry for Christ.* Paul's ministry recordings result in most of the content of our Christian Bible's New Testament. Paul's ministry experiences and recorded training instructions are for all of God's people. The instructions Paul recorded include the training for leaders of the Kingdom of God.

Paul had a great deal to learn from Jesus as he was transformed from a high level Pharisee who persecuted Christians to an anointed Apostle of Jesus Christ. God supernaturally transformed Paul from an Old Testament expert of the law and persecutor of Christians to an apostle, an ambassador and an advocate of the Gospel of Christ. Paul experienced a supernatural transformation. Just think for a moment about his family, his friends, his colleagues. How many joined him? How many ridiculed him? How many shunned Paul? We may not see ourselves the same as Paul, not as sinful, not as powerful, however, we all must experience training, spiritual enlightenment and a supernatural transformation before we can effectively serve the Kingdom of God. I am sure we are never "there" in finishing with our learning. I don't think we can achieve the ultimate level of holiness while in our flesh. We can get better every day as we keep love as the motivation of our heart and our eyes on Jesus.

It appears God is beginning to open ministry opportunities for me. I am looking forward to a new season. I know a big portion of my ministry is to train-equip leaders.

My understanding is John Wimber, a musician and charismatic pastor who started the Vineyard movement, was not a proponent of testing people to reveal their spiritual gifts. His perspective was that God will anoint our gifts as we use them to God's glory. He felt the spiritual gifts testing may limit you to just acknowledging your current gifts. I agree! Spiritual gifts are required to minister and these gifts can be added to you as you grow and as you serve God. Spiritual Gifts testing is a good measurement of your gifts on the day you take the test, however, test results will change as you learn and grow in Christ. Always keep in mind; you have potential for spiritual growth.

The Apostolic Role

Godly leaders in the Bible who were "those among the apostles," were disciples of Jesus commissioned to spread the gospel, to start ministries, to teach and to make disciples. This represents those leaders who can operate as needed in all of the fivefold gifts. When we mention a fivefold gift we are addressing the leaders of leaders-teacher of teachers gifts; i.e. Jesus' "Apostles".

The leaders who followed the direction from Christ as mentioned and referred to as the great commission in Mark 16:15-18. Their focus was to spread the news that the Messiah is here, He is alive and Jesus Christ is walking among us. Their motivation was and is clearly to multiply the kingdom of God.

Preaching, teaching the gospel, and healing the sick, raising the dead, casting out demons and teaching Kingdom principles, this is what disciples of Christ do. As we grow in our walk with Christ, we can become apostles. The Bible says Jesus is the same yesterday and today. He is still calling and making disciples and they become apostles, just as the original twelve. We know Paul was enlisted by Jesus Christ as an anointed apostle after Jesus was crucified and God raised him from the dead.

Prophetic

Am I a prophet? I have been told that I have a prophetic mantle, although I have not been recognized as a prophet. I believe that a prophetic mantle means that I have words of wisdom or knowledge from God at just the right time which will help me minister to someone. I believe the fruit of the ministry reveals the anointing and the words of God to penetrate the hearts of those to whom we minister. Prophetic words are meant to bring the disciple/mentee closer to God.

Our prophetic words from God according to 1 Corinthians 14:3, depending on the translation, should strengthen, comfort, edify and/or exhort. The words of wisdom, words of knowledge that encourage someone and let them know God loves them are prophetic words. Words from God will be backed up by the Bible. The Bible confirms that God loves us and He really wants to help.

Exhortation

The exhortation gift can be an encouragement and/or a correction. Exhortation will bring Holy Spirit conviction, not condemnation. A word from God is a word we know is not something that comes from our own minds and not something we are thinking. Prophetic words can provide direction, words of this level should come from an elder within your church fellowship; someone seasoned in God and is formally recognized as a prophet. The Bible teaches us a word from God will set us free.

Jesus was in the desert for forty days and used scripture to fight the devil and Paul was in the desert preparing for ministry for fourteen years. Fourteen years is more years than I thought would transpire in my life until God would place me in what I perceive as a more direct ministry or at least a place I really know as ministry. However I now understand that my participation in many ministries, ministries I help to start and support, is my ministry.

Apostle

Apostolic ministry for women when I was in Bible College was not on the list of available courses. It was certainly not taught it was for women. Dr. Cannistraci did allude in his book "The gift of Apostle, as I mentioned earlier, that Junia in his book may have been a woman. Apostolic ministry traditionally has simply not been addressed as a possibility for women (in some circles neither are men).

Discernment

Hebrews 5:14 states, in the King James Version, that as you grow spiritually you no longer need milk. You will discern both good and evil through all of your senses. You will discern by seeing, hearing, touching, smelling and or tasting. Discernment is a gift. It is one to be used with wisdom and should be kept in your heart/spirit until God tells you to share what you discern with anyone. Never share what you discern with anyone but the person you are ministering and your spiritual leader. I have learned that discernment is a spiritual gift used to protect you, protect your family and to protect the person to whom God has positioned you to minister.

James 1:17 teaches us that good and perfect gifts come from God. Then do all bad things come from the devil? No, not always, there are elements of both good and bad in us so some of the bad deeds are delivered by us. Bad actions, words, and thoughts can be rooted in our origin, from our flesh, our sinful nature. Our "bad" thoughts, deeds, actions can also come from bad belief systems. If we know of areas in our lives not producing the fruit of God's Spirit listed in Galatians 5:22-23 which are: "love, joy, peace, patience, kindness, goodness, faithfulness, gentleness and self-control," we should examine our hearts and repair the disconnect. After confirming the areas of our lives the fruit of God's Spirit is not evident, we need to seriously examine our beliefs, our history, our activities, and most of all, our relationships. If we cannot control a bad behavior, it may be a deliverance issue.

Only God is omnipotent, omniscient and omnipresent! Satan, the devil isn't. He does however, use two of the greatest resources of all: our minds and our mouths. The demonic can simply make a suggestion to us and trigger a thought, an experience or a bad belief system, and we can either resist it or run with it. Taking a destructive thought and not pondering the thought by measuring it against Galatians 5:22-23 because it just sounds like it could be right is a danger-stop! Don't speak a curse, even if there is substantial evidence. We are made in God's image and likeness. Our words can heal and bring life or our words can bring death and devastation. Learning to ponder is not natural for us. I am still trying to learn when to speak and when to ponder. **To ponder is not to over think, it is to be still, wait on God and to pray.**

Evangelism

We have seen Godly anointed evangelists speak and many come to Christ, adding to the kingdom of God. As opposed to an evangelist who is unorthodox in nature. An example could be a used car sales person whom doesn't care if the transaction is honorable. The only goal is making his/her quota. Our motives should always be our checkpoint. If our motive in general is love and absolutely in ministry, is love, in truth, and in advancing the kingdom of God, we are positioned to be on the right track. However, if our motives are money, greed, our ministry growth, or advancing our name, we should most likely step back. If the Holy Spirit is not the driving force, STOP!

We don't have to look for ministry; As mentioned earlier, Pastor Chris was very deliberate in this instruction. Jesus never looked for ministry; ministry found Jesus. Our Gifts make room for our call! I have heard this preached;

however, when I read Proverbs 18:16 it says *"A man's gift makes room for him, and brings him before great men."* The commentaries say this is a bribe used by a prisoner to get out of jail. If we look at this scripture we could determine a gift can be our spiritual gift(s) and the jailer can be an ungodly act or person. So from a spiritual point of view, it would appear that our gifts can make a way for us, even with the ungodly.

Chapter Four
Innovative Leadership/ Making Disciples

The title of apostle is not overly utilized nor accepted within the Christian churches I am familiar. However the title is not important; what is important is the gift. The purpose of apostolic gifts is never for acquiring admiration and fame, or drawing big crowds. A person with such gifts may acquire notoriety however they would never seek this role nor would the purpose be to bring recognition to them-self. The purpose would be to further and to strengthen the kingdom of God.

A person with apostolic gifts may find that there is favor as a result of God's unusual touch on their life; it is God that provides the person's position to build into the lives of others. It appears that God is enhancing His leadership. He appears to be introducing His leaders to a place of experiencing more of His heart in our everyday lives. Today there appears to be a greater influence or application of godly influence in all aspects of our lives. The people of God are learning how to be who we are in Christ as a part of our everyday lives. We don't preach; we should behave differently. Not because we are "special" only because we are held to a different level of accountability in all relationships. I am not implying that we are flawless. I am encouraging all of God's people to simply love all people. *Unconditional "God love"* **is the most powerful weapon** we have and unconditional love is what is needed to change this world and to overcome the impact of evil.

Godly leadership is what we are called to. To equip the saints is the role of all of the mature men and women of the church.

Disciple and Teach

As leaders, it is our job to disciple and to teach using formal or informal methods with a goal to provide the enhancement of the disciple's relationship with Christ. It is about actively enabling the knowledge transfer to those we are leading. Practical Teaching is an effective method; using Biblical standards and concepts and sharing how to apply what we learn from the Bible to all aspects of our lives.

The first step is to assess the need(s) and the goal(s). Once the goals and the needs are defined, we collaborate how to meet the needs within a mentee and or an existing ministry, or while setting up a new ministry.

Needs and Vision

Document the needs, the vision and the purpose to support ministry. Sample terms used in professional project management to identify the phases of a project/task can apply in most exercises are: initiation, planning, execution, and completion. The planning stage for new projects is typically the longest phase. If we plan first, our execution will be more focused and fruitful. The project manager may begin to work with the team to understand the problem statement (needs to be clear and concise). He/she then works with the team to brain storm the proposed solution(s). The next steps during the planning phase will be to gather an initial project team to determine: goals, objectives, risks, constraints, scope and the deliverables.

The last steps in the planning phase the Project Manager will finalize a budget and the project plan with the planned or proposed dates. The planning phase is completed after the solution, budgets, project plan and dates are approved by the stakeholders.

The execution of the project begins as the project plan is reviewed and the dates are confirmed, approved, and the required resources are identified and secured. There are many types of project plans as simple or as complex as needed to manage the project. The person leading the task/project is also responsible for reporting status; making sure the reported costs are communicated when in or out of line with the budget and monitoring the over and under-utilization of required resources.

Resources may include contractors, money, machines, people and time. The Project Manager is responsible for continued communication and updating the project's progress. They are also responsible for documenting and distributing the meeting minutes and the reporting of achievements and issues that are impacting the progress of the project. The follow up with the project team is crucial and necessary to support a successful project. These project management concepts work and can apply in most every task or aspect of our lives, including ministry

The completion stage is used to identify when the implementation of the deliverables are ready. This time is used to analyze and review the final budget vs. actual expenditures and to collect and document the lessons learned. Communication and planning are crucial to the success of any project. Communication is 95 percent of a project manager's job. If we are to serve God as leaders, we are required to be consistent, responsible and to communicate to our teams.

Integrity

Do not make promises you cannot or do not keep. You will lose your credibility as a leader if your word (what you say or commit to do) is not valued. We represent God in all we do. If we cannot be trusted, we make God look bad. It is important to keep a calendar to make sure you do not over commit. Hurting people come to a church for healing. If the person is ministering to them forgets something he/she promised, the people will in many cases leave the church and then their hurt is directed not only to the leader, their disappointment can be directed to God. An apostolic leader is not perfect; however, there are many tools we can use to better communicate with our teams. Your integrity as a leader within a leadership role is crucial.

Mentoring/ Discipling can be as formal as a team lead or as informal as a close friendship. Relationships are built with those we mentor. Mentees are the persons we support and encourage in leading a Godly life. Mentoring is for the elder (not necessarily chronologically older). An apostolic mentor can be a person Biblically trained to equip the younger mentee (mentee can be a new adult Christian) and to coach the disciple/mentee on how to grow closer to Jesus. We are encouraged to consistently improve relationships, learning Biblical principles and how to apply these principles in all aspects of life. Becoming more like Jesus is our daily goal.

The chronological age of a mentor is typically older in years but it is not required. Experience in years within a function of a recognized or known gift could merit mentoring. Mentoring focus is to enable the mentee so he/she may maximize their personal and ministry potential and develop the skills typically already accomplished and realized by the mentor. The mentee should show signs of improved performance and become better at a skill and as a Godly person. An apostolic person would want to encourage and help support the mentee/disciple into ultimately answering their call, their ministry.

Keep Growing

Mentors do not know it all! We continue to learn. I am kinesthetic, I learn by doing. I have learned more from teaching because of the discipline required while preparing the training material. We will never know it all (when we know it all, we need God less) and we must have a desire to continue to grow in our relationship with God as we mentor/ disciple.

Coaching

The role of a coach is observing the person in action or listening to a mentee or disciple during or providing input after a situation or life occurrence. The disciple or mentee may request the coach to provide input and or request needed direction during or after the practical application. Unsolicited advice while coaching or correcting should be done in love, have biblical precedence, and it should be encouraging and constructive. Remember a prophetic word from God will comfort, edify and or exhort.

I have noted some of the areas I have experienced and acknowledge as important. It is paramount we facilitate the mentee's exploration of their own needs in their relationship with God through Jesus Christ. Each relationship with God is a personal relationship.

God is no respecter of persons; however, just as multiple children have multiple needs, God knows our needs and He loves us individually. Jer. 1:5 "Before I formed you in the womb I knew you, and before you were born I consecrated you; I have appointed you a prophet to the nations."

The mentor checks the mentee to be sure they keep their motivation clearly set on love. The individual's desires must always be reviewed and determined if they are of the world or are the desires that God has placed in their hearts. The Bible has all of the answers. The person's experiences and their skills will influence their thought process. Our role is to always send them to the Bible-to God to assist the individual in making a real and a lasting change. We cannot change a person. Only growing in their relationship with God will institute change. We can lead them to Him in what we say, what we do, how we instruct, and how we live our life. You cannot just teach if you do not live what you are teaching.

Support the mentee in setting appropriate goals and methods of assessing progress toward these goals. Watch, listen, and ask questions to understand the situation.

Resources

The Bible will be our greatest resource; there are also many Christian books and ministries that may be included in our one-on-one training, facilitating, counseling and networking. Prayerfully consider where God is leading you.

Commitment

Encourage a commitment to God and the development of a lasting personal relationship with Christ; a relationship that includes continual growth and change. The Coach should always maintain an unconditionally loving and positive heart for the mentee which means that the coach is at all times supportive and non-judgmental of the person and their past experiences. We don't judge a person based on their past, however, we understand that their experiences will impact their views. Their past lifestyle is history. Keep encouraging a bright future, encourage aspirations in their new walk with Christ. Encourage a Christian to develop his/her personal competencies in hearing from God. Do not develop unhealthy dependencies on the coaching or mentoring relationship. Remind ourselves that Jesus is the Savior, not the person acting as the mentor/coach.

Evaluate and measure the milestones of the mentoring process. Use objective measures wherever possible to ensure the mentee's relationship with God is improving and the mentee is achieving some of their personal goals. Encourage your mentees/disciples to continually improve their knowledge of areas to minister, enhancing their competencies of the word of God, emulating the ministry of Jesus and develop their own new relationships/partnerships where necessary to achieve God's ministry goals. Our goals are achieved as long as they produce the fruit of God's Spirit; as I previously mentioned. Goals measured by the fruit of God's Spirit will produce the following; love, joy, peace, patience, kindness, goodness, faithfulness, gentleness and self-control.

Coaching can only be accomplished when the mentor works within their area of personal competence and anointing. Each coach/mentor must possess qualifications and experience in the areas in which the coaching is offered. A pastor I heard once said if you want to grow in your relationship with God and to learn how to minister at a greater level, find someone you admire and can confirm success in the ministry area you have a desire to learn and where you could possibly serve. Serving in a ministry is a great way to get involved and to learn from those you know are successful in their service of God. How will you know them? Jesus taught that we will know them by their fruits.

"You will know them by their fruits. Do men gather grapes from thorn bushes or figs from thistles?...Therefore <u>by their fruits you will know them</u>"(Matthew 7:16, 20).

Transparency

Transparency is important for the mentor and the mentee. No one but Jesus is perfect. Paul wrote in Romans 3:23 "for all have sinned and fall short of the glory of God." The mentor should not share everything he/she has experienced. This is not a counseling time for the mentor; however, sharing enough to put the mentee at ease is recommended. Finding areas of our life experience that we can share in common is a great way to connect. Emphasis on confidentiality between the mentee and the mentor is advised.

Building trust will make a great impact. However, the mentor should be sure when the connection begins that he/she advises the mentee that if there is any endangerment or inappropriate treatment of a child discussed by the mentee, it may be reported to your leadership. If there was abuse experienced by the mentee, however and the mentee is legally an adult the requirement to report to the leadership can be optional. However it is advised while counseling with the mentee that he/she connect to resources you know will encourage healing.

Correction

Correction is never fun and should be taken seriously. It is important for leaders to correct when necessary. Pastor Chris stated that while teaching, discipline performed without love is abuse. I have found that there is no better measure than the motivation of our heart. If you check your motives and you correct a person in love, hopefully it will be received in love. When you care about the person and their positive growth, ignoring an area to be corrected is wrong and can grow into resentment. Certainly it is not advisable to react quickly nor in anger. I have learned walking away, sleeping on it, and prayer helps me to deliver a much more effective and meaningful correction.

Exhortation

Exhortation is one of the gifts recorded in Romans 12. Given a choice of encouraging by empathy or encouraging by *exhortation*, a person with this motivational gift will *exhort*.

An exhorter's **basic motivational drive is to encourage believers to mature in Christ** and to grow spiritually. Exhorters often seek to stimulate development by teaching, counseling, and discipling others. Pleasing God is more important to an exhorter than pleasing the mentee.

Unconventional Living

Not status quo: *definition is "the existing state of affairs, especially regarding social or political issues."* A person with an apostolic call may live an unconventional life. I have found for most of my life, I don't seem to fit. I am not special. In fact, I am not always sure exactly why I am here. I am convinced that God is the only one who can fulfill the desires of my heart.

Joy

I know beyond a shadow of a doubt God that has called me to lead, train, exhort and to love His leaders. But lately I hear God saying "I want you to have joy in your life, where is your joy"? This question has been difficult to answer. I am not a martyr; however I am so programmed to take care of things. I have learned that I am not programmed for joy. I am learning with God, joy is available and required. I know Gal. 5:22-23 lists joy as one of the fruits of God's Spirit. I cried when God first asked me the question, because I was not sure how to respond. It had not occurred to me that I could or should **live in joy**. I have found that teaching, leading projects and serving God in ministries is where I experience the most day to day joy.

Live in Joy? Wow, joy is something to ponder; the most joyful times in my life were when my daughter was born and when my spiritual daughters Stephanie and Heather joined my life. I had great joy when I was in Bible College. Joy when I participated in the Freedom Clinic, and when we started the SARAH Ministry. I had great joy ministering healing and deliverance for the five years I was a lay pastor at Evangel. My granddaughter is an amazing joy in my life. I have enjoyed supporting ministries. But I cannot say that in the past five years there has been a great deal of real living in joy.

I can think of a sweet and spontaneous joy when Sophia (Steph's daughter) out of the blue, kissed me on the cheek when we were reading; this was a joy filled moment.

I had great joy in the first few years in contract manufacturing. I loved leading the training team, traveling to other countries with Heather, working crazy hours on projects and in the midst of the projects going into conference rooms and praying for team members. We were a bit crazy when late one evening we decided to prayer walk in downtown Guadalajara. It was exciting to explore Mexico, Paris, Hungary and China while learning so much about other cultures. Heather will always be one of my spiritual daughters. I pray for her and truly love her unconditionally. Heather's family has grown and since relocated to the Dallas area. I consider her family as my extended family, I am blessed.

Chapter Five

Apostolic Team Building

Team building, practical project teams, ministry teams work well and are able to meet needs quicker and more effectively as a team.

Steps to consider while forming a team:

1. Identify the team's purpose, examples:
    a. Board of Directors
    b. Building projects
    c. Church Plant
    d. Mission Trips
    e. Schools
2. Determine the charter, task and or the ministry focus, examples:
    a. Building Homes, Schools
    b. Drilling wells to supply clean fresh water
    c. Feeding Children
    d. Parenting the orphans
    e. Recovery: abuse, addictions, divorce, etc.

f. Singles recovery, divorce, death of a spouse
g. Single Parenting
h. Understanding and meeting the needs of a People Group
i. Women and Children

*"Pure and genuine religion in the sight of God the Father means caring for **orphans** and **widows** in their distress and refusing to let the world corrupt you"* (James 1:27).

Ministry Teams

The ministry team members are formed and chosen based on their passions, gifts and experience. Team members are placed in a team to strengthen each other and their community/people group.

Ministry teams encourage spiritual growth, while working together building relationships, complementing and supporting God's plan for the individuals and the ministry. While preparing to minister as a team, accountability is not only encouraged, it is required. In most ministry leadership accountability is assumed; however it should be noted and defined within the team. Leaders most often need to provide permission to their team members to deliver and to accept correction and to receive exhortation as God ordains.

All team members should be trained in biblical counseling and healing, able to discern, recognize symptoms, and lead to Biblical solutions. Solutions most often begin with forgiveness, as many issues can be rooted in unforgiveness; while enabling the awareness of each person's or the team's prophetic destiny, preparing for their God given appointment. Praying and seeking God together enables this process to begin and the healing to happen. Each person's destiny will vary as each individual's needs are met through their intimate relationship with Jesus.

Perfection will never be realized on this earth; however there are reasons God encourages unity. Ministering together as a team, working together and praying together, praying for each other is how we get closer to God's design for our lives.

Stop, Drop, and Pray

There is a saying that Christians eat their own [consider this an exhortation]. Let's change the saying to *"Christians love, take care of, and defend their own."* When we hear our brother or sister has made a mistake we need to stop immediately, drop to our knees and pray. Judgment needs to be the furthest from our minds. If we are tempted to judge, we need to remember we are to give and to receive grace. If we truly love our brothers and sisters, praying for them should be our first reaction.

When my granddaughter was born at 25 weeks gestation, she weighed one pound and seven ounces. My immediate reaction was to go to God and plead for her life and her health. I didn't check to see if my praying for her protection and her healthy survival was okay with anyone. Just think what our world would be like if we did not hesitate to go to God and to pray for each other.

Teams will learn to encourage each other how to live life more abundantly (John 10:10), making Jesus' reason for dying worth the price He paid on the cross. In living a life pleasing to God and producing good fruit from our lives, we should realize what it means to *live in joy*, live in love, and to live in peace, treat others in kindness, display goodness in our actions, words and deeds, consistently providing patience and self- control.

Chapter Six
Sending and Releasing

A postolos (Apostle) has a stronger sense than the word *messenger*, meaning one who is entrusted with a foreign mission, with the authority of a delegate. In the Greek version of the Old Testament it occurs once, in 1 Kings, 14:6 The English translation is "I am sent to you . . .", or "I have been commissioned to give you . . ."

Team Direction

The purpose of apostolic team ministry is combining team members with a strong combination of spiritual and practical gifts/talents, while making disciples and releasing them as a team into their call to appreciate their prophetic destiny. We do this by training, promoting and sending the team members into their area of ministry, prepared and ready to further the Kingdom of God.

We are servants of God. In Matthew 10:8, Matthew 28:18-20, and Mark 16 we are all commissioned and instructed to *"Heal the sick, cleanse the lepers, raise the dead, and cast out demons. Freely you have received, freely give"*. Jesus sent the apostles initially to the people of Israel. Thank God Paul was sent to minister to the Gentiles. We are expected to carry on in the name of Jesus. Jesus gave us the authority saying. *"Behold, I give you the authority to trample on serpents and scorpions, and over all the power of the enemy, and nothing shall by any means hurt you"* (Luke 10:19).

We are commissioned to make disciples to teach and to mentor just like Jesus. Apostolic Ministry is making disciples. It is to equip the body of Christ, motivating and exemplifying unconditional love, and living a life in child-like trust in God.

The ministry in which we participate is not our ministry, it is God's ministry. If we hold on too tightly, there is danger that the ministry will become our ministry and not God's ministry. If ministry becomes stale and if there is no fruit, it is time to seriously consider stepping back to listen to God and receive God's instruction. Our identity is not what we do, our identity is determined in who we are in Christ. Our motivation is love for God first and people second.

During a Breath of Heaven leader's offsite meeting, we watched a video of Lester Sumrall. He was a very powerful Pentecostal evangelist who preached over 55 years in 110 countries. He was coaching a young evangelist. Toward the end of this young man's sermon, Lester approached him and whispered in his ear, "Son, the Holy Spirit left about a half hour ago, I suggest you do the same." Wow, now you have our attention.

Chapter Seven

Practical Application

If you don't believe in the promises of God you will rely on your own fears. Proclaim God's promises and His Faithfulness before man, so God gets the glory.

God is faithful to deliver what He has promised.

> *"But if God so clothes the grass in the field, which is alive today and tomorrow is thrown into the furnace, how much more will He clothe you? You men of little faith"* (Luke 12:28).

I am convinced that nothing of this world can keep me from what God has called me to, but me.

My prayer, my petition to God, is to place on my heart and on the heart of my leaders what He wants for me. I pray God binds me to His will and His plan for my life. Bless me, oh God, and make me a blessing!

God's promises to practice:

Jeremiah 29:11 NIV: *"For I know the plans I have for you," declares the* L<small>ORD</small>, *"plans to **prosper you** and not to harm you, plans to give you **hope and a future**."*

Matthew 11:28-29: *"Come to me, all you who are weary and burdened, and **I will give you rest**...."*

Philippians 4:19: *"And this same **God who takes care of me will supply all your needs** from his glorious riches, which have been given to us in Christ Jesus."*

Romans 8:38-39: *"For I am persuaded **that neither death** nor life, nor **angels** nor **principalities nor powers**, nor things present nor **things to come**, nor **height nor depth**, nor any other **created thing**, shall be able to **separate us from the love of God** which is in Christ Jesus our Lord."*

Proverbs 1:33: *"But all who listen to me will **live in peace**..."*

John 14:27: *Peace I leave with you, My peace I give to you; not as the world gives do I give to you. Let not your heart be troubled,* **neither let it be afraid.**

Romans 10:9: *"If you confess with* **your mouth** *that* **Jesus is Lord** *and* **believe in your heart** *that God raised him from the dead* **you will be saved.**"

When I was laid off the end of January 2014, strangely, I was excited. Excited to be free of a job that I had tried so hard to like and excited about where God was leading me for the next phase of my life. I have been unemployed for 5 months. I have written this book. I have cleaned my home, reorganized almost every closet, drawer and cabinet. I have thrown away and donated so that I am almost down to the essentials (well not exactly). God has given me a new vision and a new focus. I believe God is encouraging me to not give up on my dreams, but to collaborate with Him in this new adventure in a life He is now ordaining.

Fifteen and a half years ago, I graduated from Bible College. Our vision was to start a church, but it didn't happen. It was difficult to not be discouraged. I heard Bill Johnson say a few years ago, discouragement is partnering with a spirit of unbelief. Discouragement is a feeling we need to replace with faith that God has a plan and in His plan we will prosper. *Hebrews 13:5 "Let your conduct be without covetousness: be content with such things as you have. For He Himself has said,* **"I will never leave you nor forsake you."** It is God's word hidden in our hearts so we avoid sin and so we can trust God. We must have faith.

When our perceived vision to start a church failed I thought my change in focus was to work, make money and fund ministries. My heart was also to fund children's education. However I am now challenged by God to not only find my joy, but to **live in joy**. Joy comes from ministry and the presence of God. In Acts 13:52, *"And the disciples were filled with joy and with the Holy Spirit."* Acts 15:3, *'So, being sent on their way by the church, they passed through Phoenicia and Samaria, describing the conversion of the Gentiles; and they caused great joy to all the brethren."*

My joy is when I am teaching, leading projects and leading others into a closer relationship with God. I find joy in mentoring, organizing, setting up, reorganizing; while encouraging God's people to recognize their gifts and to challenge them to live in the authority Christ has given us, living a life positioned for blessing. In John 10:10 we read, *"Jesus said he came that we would live life more abundantly."* Let's make Jesus' reasons for coming worth what He went through to reconcile us to God.

What Now?

Praying, preparing and believing my God will open doors to the job and the ministry He has ready just for me (or you).

The ministry He has selected specifically for me (or you) to participate and possibly to lead. We are always in full time ministry whether we have a secular job or within a specific known Christian ministry. Our eyes should always be fixed upon God as we prepare for a position on a ministry team. Your passions will direct you to the equipping right for you. If you desire to learn more about what God has for you, find a Bible College. I went to Bible College to learn more about the Bible; I had no idea I might have a call in God's kingdom.

Women in Church Leadership

In the church where I grew up, women were not allowed in general to lead, to preach, and to teach everyone. The business world has used me in leadership. I now know God has always had a place for me in His leadership. He will make a way for me. He will place me on the hearts of those He wants to value, recognize and to use me.

There are practical Bible Colleges geared to in-depth Bible study, prayer, counseling and leadership training. Find the classes in your church community. American Association Christian Counselors is also a wonderful training tool for Christian counseling. I took "Caring for People God's Way," it was wonderful. Many of us (including me) needed counseling so this course became another step in my healing and in my growth in Christ.

Write down all of your skills and experiences in any area of business and ministry. Some examples are: advertising, budgeting, customer service, facilities, finance, leadership (if you are a parent you are leader), marketing, planning, procurement, project management, and sales. All of these gifts/skills are what is needed to operate within a ministry team.

How Will You Apply This to What You Know of Your Purpose?

What is your passion, what are your recognized gifts, your practical skills? If your job is in sales and marketing, you may be an evangelist. If your passion is training-educating, you could be a fivefold teacher. If you have a heart to love, counsel and to lead people, you could be a pastor. If you cannot stop speaking the truth by exhorting, comforting and edifying others, you could be a prophet. If you enjoy the setup and hiring of a new business, a new department, organizing a team, or reorganizing when there have been challenges you may have an apostolic call. The practical application of who you are and what you do will reveal your call by God, His anointing will attract others to you.

Where Do You Fit?

We all have a place in the body of Christ. Find and attend a church. Show your willingness to be consistent, reliable and a person others can count on when needed. Obey God's word. Trust God and simply love people. Pray, pray, pray!!!

Humility

No one person has all of the answers. We are all a part of the body of Christ. We all have a function needed to comprise a ministry team. The Apostle, the Prophet, the Evangelist, the Pastor and the Teacher comprise the fivefold ministry. God can place you anywhere He chooses. Your choices can lead you in a direction toward a ministry call; one that will bless you and will bless those you minister. Don't let the doctrine of man inhibit your growth in Christ Jesus. Seeking God's call for you is individual and is specific to you. Knowing the Bible, hearing God's voice, spending time with Him will guide you in the direction you should go. How do you know if you're on the right path? As I have previously mentioned, if it is of God, your life will produce the fruit of God's Spirit listed in Galatians 5:22-23.

Chapter Eight
Next Steps

I have been told I am in the desert or is it the wilderness? The last three years have been the most uncomfortable in my life's experience. It is dry and hot in the desert. The good part of a desert experience is that there is supernatural sustenance from God. Yes, there has been murmuring, forgive me Lord; however, now I have a glimpse of the promise land. I know that starting the prayer ministry training at InRoads Church has been my crossing of the Jordan. I know there is milk and honey on the other side. There are more ministries and more fruit, with our needs met by his riches and glory. I am not naïve of the giants; however, I know we will fight them together.

I have a vision to share, a vision of practical ministry training. Not Bible College, we have Bible colleges for those who are called to be full time pastors/priests as were the Levites. A practical ministry vision of ministry teams taught the Biblical answers to prayer, healing, counseling, relationships, provision, unity, conflict resolution, etc. How our needs are to be met by God's riches and glory. This school can be within a church or a community ministry with Biblical teaching, supported by a team called to training and equipping the body of Christ.

We are not all pastors/priests, however, we need to know how to minister and seek God for ourselves, for our families and for our community. Biblical prayer and counseling those in need will be a byproduct of this training. The training will teach the body of Christ how to get closer to God. Sunday school is not as prevalent today and does not appear to be a standard part of the recent church experience. In our culture, people are too busy and individual churches do not always have the resources needed within one congregation. We need to equip the whole body of Christ, to make the church strong.

Conclusion

All of God's people must be free to serve Him. Women of God need to freely serve God to fulfill their destiny and to help strengthen the family of God. If you are a parent, you are a leader. If you are married, you are a member of a team and you are a leader. If you are single, God is your mate and you are a team with the best team leader.

How does God feel about His people not assuming their roles within His Kingdom? How does God feel about anyone not being allowed to be who He has designed them to be? Ponder these questions as it pertains to you.

In Judges, we learn that Deborah was an anointed Judge, a great leader of God's people, and we also learn about Jael who was what seems to be the equivalent of a house wife in today's terms. The Biblical account records how they saved God's people. In Judges 4:21 we learn how Jael killed Sisera, the lead of the enemy's army, the Canaanite chieftain. Barak, the general of Israel's army came by Jael's camp in pursuit of Sisera; Jael took him to her tent where she reveals the demise of Sisera. We learn from this story to never underestimate the wisdom and the power of a woman when put in a position to protect her family. Israel was blessed and the war was stopped by both Deborah and Jael as they accepted and assumed their call by God.

Esther, too, saved God's people from imminent annihilation. Mary, the mother of Jesus was certainly a leader of leaders as she raised our Savior. My mom used to say how women should be revered, because our God chose a 15 year old virgin girl to bring our savior into this world. How wonderful it would be to learn how to ponder from Mary. There have been many women God has chosen to lead His people to physical and spiritual salvation. The Bible and many other historical books detail their roles in the Kingdom of God.

What Should You Do?

List your passions, locate someone mature in the ministry you are compelled to pursue, and find training for your ministry. How will you know you are there? You will find your joy resides in your call from God.

God loves you and He is calling you to be closer to Him and to realize your full potential in Christ. Don't disqualify yourself! *"Therefore, do not be ashamed of the testimony about our Lord, nor of me his prisoner, but share in suffering for the gospel by the power of God, who saved us **and called us to a holy calling, not because of our works but because of his own purpose and grace,** which he gave us in Christ Jesus before the ages began"* (2 Timothy 1:8).

My Prayer is that this book will bring all of you the encouragement you need to seek God for His specific plans for you.

> Dear God,
>
> *Jeremiah 29:11 states, "For I know the plans I have for you," declares the LORD, "plans to prosper you and not to harm you, plans to give you hope and a future."*
>
> Show me where to find my joy in You. Keep my eyes fixed upon you Jesus. Make Your vision, my vision. Keep my heart, my mind, my will and my emotions in sync with You.
>
> Lord, please reveal Your plan for me. Open the doors you have ordained for me. Please make my path clear, lead me to Your purpose for this time of my life. My hope is in You, my future is in You. Make me a blessing as you continue to bless me. Your word says you will

prosper me, you will protect me. You will never harm me. I have your promises in my heart; I will carry You in my heart to eternity.

In the name of Jesus, Amen

Addendum

Practical Ministry Training for Everyone!

Goal: Training all of God's people - Eph. 4:11

Three to Six bimonthly training Sessions

Goals:

- Identifying and building leadership teams
- Training leaders how to recognize and make disciples.
- Encouraging practical biblical teachings and how to apply the word of God to our daily lives.

Training Examples:
- AACC Caring for People God's Way
- Accountability
- Building Relationships (how to bless and to be a blessing)
- Covenant (the meaning and how it works in God's Kingdom)
- Communication with God & each other
- Daily Bible & Prayer (the importance and application of staying close to God)

- Discipleship
- Discipline, Correction (what is healthy, what is abuse)
- Dreams & Visions
- Encounters (quarterly?): Healing & Deliverance
- Finding our Purpose-Who we are in Christ
- Kingdom Principles
- Motivation, Defining what motivates you (money, perfection, love, serving God)
- What is God, what is the enemy, what is the driving force influencing my desires.
    - Is it the enemy; is it God or my selfish desires?
- Prayer Accommodating, a safe place to pray
- Prayer Ministry Counseling
- Prayer Team Ministry Training, Committed to the advancement of the Kingdom
- Angry at God; ministry to angry people
- Discernment, Hebrews 5:14-how to mature and use this gift wisely
- Hiding from God? Why do we hide from our healer?
- Knowing our authority
- Pride & Shame how are they connected? (Proverbs 11:2)
- What happens when we pray?
- Prophetic; edify-comfort-exhort (speaking life into our family, friends, community)
- Serving at the Pleasure of the King (what does this mean)
- What is God's Will
- Worship (how to enter into the presence of God)

Diana's Ministry Related Bio:

1995-2000 Diana a member of Evangel Christian Fellowship became a lay pastor and was asked to supervise the healing and recovery ministries and act as the director of the Freedom Clinic. In December of 1998, Diana graduated from Evangel's Impact School of Ministry. She later attained her Associates in Practical Ministry from Wagner Leadership Institute.

December of 2000 Diana returned to Fremont Community Church. Diana felt God was encouraging her to return to FCC to share what she had learned. The pastoral leadership was very affirming and supported her. It was a great time of reestablishing relationships and meeting new people and making new friends, while sharing what she learned about The Holy Spirit, ministry and the Bible. The team's vision during this time was to start a Biblical Counseling Prayer Center. She received Certification "Caring for People God's Way" AACC (American Association of Christian Counselors). This vision has not yet been realized.

2001-2009 Diana joined a global contract manufacturing corporation. She was promoted to Director within the Information Technology Department. Diana has led and supported many projects as she traveled extensively to many US locations, Europe, Mexico, South America and Asia. Her ministry is where she is and during this time it was in the workplace.

2007–2011 Diana became a member of Jubilee Christian Center, she was on the Board of Directors responsible for the operations of Breath of Heaven Ministries; later ACTs Worldwide. She worked within the ministry leadership team to train leaders, raise funds, lead mission trips and manage projects for drilling of wells in Tanzania and providing funds to send orphans to school. In Kenya, the projects provided a fresh water system as well as, building the foundation and the first floor of an orphans home and school.

2012-2014 Diana's passion is serving Christ as He continues to be the focus of her life. She is the Chairman of the Board for Pregnancy Choices Clinic in Union City and a member of InRoads Church in Fremont. Diana is on the board for the women's ministry within InRoads and is responsible for equipping.

In the summer of 2014, the Women's Ministry Prayer Team Training was started. Answered prayer began the first week. God continues to bless us with answers to prayers. The answers are incredible. Jodi Harris, the pastor's wife shared in the second meeting her praise report, the prayers for God's will and direction for a job and a home were answered. The answers to her prayers were even greater than what was articulated.

The most important attribute of Christian leadership is loving people. Diana resides in Fremont, California. She is active in her community as a participant of the Tri Cities CityServe Intercession team. She is very close to her extended family, her daughter, son in-law, granddaughter, brother, sister in-law and her nephew and niece. God has also blessed Diana with spiritual children whom she loves and keeps in prayer.

God has placed on Diana's heart a call to disciple, mentor, and to equip-train leaders. God has given her the insight to recognize and to build into the practical and spiritual lives of leaders. In her job and her ministry, she encourages leaders to support their team to look out for each other. Success is achieved when the team completes the task on time while supplying the customer's deliverables. When serving God we are serving His people and building His team. While serving as a Godly leader, her emphasis is **hearing from God and discernment while acknowledging and exercising the power of prayer.**

July 27th of 2014 Diana moved to Texas.

Contact the Author

Diana Graham
diagram.tex@gmail.com
(972) 459-7129